Write Well

Mark P. Painter

Jarndyce & Jarndyce Press
Cincinnati Book Publishers

Jarndyce & Jarndyce Press
Cincinnati Book Publishers
www.cincybooks.com

© 2007 by Mark P. Painter. All rights reserved.
Cartoons © Marc Tyler Nobleman,
www.mtncartoons.com, used by permission
Design by Mark P. Painter
Printed by John S. Swift Co., Inc., Cincinnati
Printed in the United States of America
First Edition, May 2007

ISBN 978-0-9772720-2-0

Dedication

My wife, Sue Ann Painter, an author herself (*Architecture in Cincinnati: An Illustrated History of Designing and Building an American City*; *William Henry Harrison: Father of the West*), suggested this book. She has edited my non-legal work for more than 20 years. This book is dedicated to her.

Mark P. Painter
May 2007

www.judgepainter.org

"If I had time, I would write a shorter letter."

—Blaise Pascal,
sometimes attributed to Mark Twain
who probably said it too.

Contents

Acknowledgments 13
How We Got Into This Mess 15
Rules 18
Rule 1 19
   Know Your Audience
Rule 2 21
   Front-Load Your Document—
   Context before Detail
Rule 3 23
   Frame the Issue in Fewer than 75 Words
Rule 4 25
   State the Facts Succinctly
Rule 5 26
   Avoid Overchronicling—Most Dates Are Clutter
Rule 6 27
   No Parenthetical Numerals
Rule 7 30
   Headings Are Signposts—They Should Inform
Rule 8 32
   Write Short Paragraphs
Rule 9 35
   Form is Important—Make it Look Good
Rule 10 39
   Edit, Edit, Edit

The 1818 Rule 41
Rule 11 41
Write Short Sentences—the 1818 Rule, Part I
Rule 12 45
Use Mainly Active Voice—the 1818 Rule, Part II
Rule 13 50
Use *But* and *And* to Begin Sentences
Rule 14 54
Distinguish Between *That* and *Which*
Rule 15 56
Use the Dash, Parenthesis, and
Comma for Degrees of Emphasis
Rule 16 58
One Word Is Usually Enough
Rule 17 63
Hyphenate Phrasal Adjectives
Rule 18 64
Always Question *Of*
Rule 19 66
Use the Serial Comma
Rule 20 67
Avoid Unnecessary Preambles
Rule 21 69
You May Split Infinitives—
But Not Often
Rule 22 70
Commas and Periods
Go Inside Quotes—Always

Rule 23 74
　Use Lists to Simplify
Rule 24 76
　Use the Possessive Before Gerunds
Rule 25 78
　Remember the Reader
We Can Do Better 80
Bibliography 81
Biography 82
Order Blank 88

Acknowledgments

My affair with plain-language legal writing began when I attended a seminar given by Bryan Garner in 1995. It was a revelation. Not that my writing had been awful before that and is great now, but I now understand so much more about written communication.

At our court, we have an editor who pores over every opinion. I strive to receive as few corrections as possible, but I have never gotten a perfect score. Christopher Dietz was also kind enough to review this work on his own time, and I appreciate his comments and corrections. Any errors are, of course, mine.

My wife, Sue Ann Painter, also read the work before publication. She was able to offer insights from a different perspective—she is a cultural historian, editor, and author of three books.

Tony Brunsman, of Cincinnati Book Publishing, handles marketing for many books and authors. He does so well that two editions of my legal writing book sold out quickly.

Jan Jolley of John S. Swift has handled the production and printing of most of my books. She is a delight to work with.

How We Got into this Mess

American writing is not good. Though there are certainly many exceptions, many of us have trouble with even rudimentary written communication. And it doesn't help that we see bad examples every day: some newspapers, many signs, countless websites, some books. How did this happen? Let's start at the beginning.

Where did we learn to write? Grammar school is certainly not that any more; but we learned rudimentary rules in grade school. Unfortunately, some of those "rules" were not rules at all.

The grade-school teacher who told you not to start a sentence with *and* really meant not to write "I have a dog. And a cat. And a parakeet." Those are not sentences. So the "rule" was just shorthand for making us write in complete sentences. The trouble is that no one disabused us of this notion later. As I will discuss later, the use of *and* and *but* to begin a sentence is one mark of good writing.

And you can, but not often, split an infinitive. "To boldly go where no one has gone before" would not read or sound the same without the infinitive split.

Likewise, there never has been any stricture against ending a sentence with a preposition. Do so when necessary. We have all seen sentences in which the writer strains to avoid the sentence-ending preposition, resulting in a weird construction: "She is a delight with which to work," rather than "She is a delight to work with." Winston Churchill is alleged to have said "That is a rule up with which I will not put."

Some of us honed our writing skills in high school and college. We learned from reading examples of good literature and other forms of writing—from journalistic to persuasive. Unless we fell victim to academic-jargon illiteracy (a subject for a separate treatise), we usually got better with practice. Though we may still have been handicapped by some false rules from grade school, some of us became at least passable writers.

Then we got worse. We stopped writing much for a while. Early jobs might not have required much writing. Some of us stopped reading much—it wasn't required. And a lot of what we did read was itself poorly written—think technical or instruction manuals.

The theme of this short book is writing in plain language. The plain-language movement has many champions, and is slowly winning over professionals in all walks of life. Even lawyers and judges are beginning to sign on to the theory.

Bryan Garner, the noted lecturer on legal writing and author of many books on writing in general, is my personal hero. You should always keep his book *Dictionary of American Usage* on your desk. It is now the standard reference for American English usage. The book has a section on false grammar rules, which Garner calls "superstitions."

Writing is a skill that can be learned—not that any of us can learn to be a Shakespeare, Steinbeck, or Holmes—or Elmore Leonard. But we don't normally need to write great fiction. We need to write business or professional communication. And we can substantially improve our communication by learning a few skills, a few tricks, and unlearning some "rules" that get in the way of good writing.

Rules of Writing

In this book I propose 25 rules to improve your writing. It's an arbitrary number—there could be 500. Because this is a primer, I have limited it to a manageable number. And though some discussion of grammar is necessary, it's not a grammar book.

I use "rules" because that seems about midway between "laws" and "suggestions." They are not laws, because some can be broken, and many must be fit to the specific task. But you should know why you are breaking them. They are a bit more than suggestions—many you may ignore only at your peril.

Rule 1
Know Your Audience

In all writing, as in speaking, the first rule is to know your audience. If you are communicating to a friend about an upcoming outing, your tone will be much less formal than if your are applying for a job, or a loan, or presenting a proposal to your boss.

Who are you writing for? Are you writing for someone who already knows a lot about the subject, or do you have to explain all the facts, and maybe the terms, from scratch. Obviously, you would not write the same way to these different audiences.

Is your writing explanatory—trying to explain something? Or is it persuasive—trying to persuade someone to do what you propose? Do you want the reader to be able to fix the laptop, or buy one?

Think about your audience. What is their education level? What do they already know about the subject? You already know a lot about your subject, but the reader does not. Avoid the temptation to start in the middle, assuming the readers know as much as you do.

"Is that just a suggestion, or really more of a law?"

Rule 2
Front-Load Your Document — Context Before Detail

Too many memos, letters, reports, and other documents start out by stating the facts. That is a mistake. Unless you are writing a mystery, do not leave the reader wondering where you are going. Do not start out giving facts without giving the context. Organize your document to be front-loaded; that is, educate the reader as to what is coming.

Readers understand much more easily if they have a context. Because readers understand new information in relation to what they already know, tell them a piece of new information that relates to their presumed knowledge. Put the important material up front. Then build on that information with each new piece you add.

And ask yourself how much your audience already knows about your subject. What do you have to tell them first?

If you are writing for a Michigan audience, you can just write *snow*, and people will understand immediately that it is a white, cold, beautiful, and often troublesome substance. If you write about snow to a Samoan, you might have to explain it.

You must build a container—context—in the reader's mind, so when you pour in the facts of your writing, the reader has the container to hold the information. Otherwise, it leaks out.

And put the container right up front. The next rule will tell you how.

Rule 3
Frame the Issue in Fewer than 75 Words

Let's assume you are writing a proposal to your boss, suggesting that the company buy a certain type of widget. You have done your research and have discovered that the company can save thousands of dollars by switching to this type of widget.

Before you start in with facts, or anything else, tell the reader what the proposal is about. The most important part of your proposal, memorandum, or whatever is framing the issue. What do you want the reader to know, and to *do*?

Do not start writing until you have a succinct statement of what you are writing about. And you must do this in 50-75 words. If you can't explain the issue in 75 words, you do not understand it very well, and neither will your reader. Put your issue statement right up front, preferably in the first paragraph.

In our widget example, you could start this way:

> I have done extensive research on the cost of widgets to our company. We now use ABX No.

38765ztr widget, manufactured by ABX Inc. We have been doing business with ABX for six years. My research studied four other widgets that all have the same performance capabilities: Bartleby model 48574857, Zirco model GT67Fz, Bient Co. model VVVx90, and Fastwig model 4. As a result I have determined. . ..

Or you could start this way:

Our company could save $560,000 per year if we switch widgets. We now use ABX No. 38765ztr. If we change to Fastwig model 4, we will get the same performance for much less money.

Which is more persuasive? Which will the boss be most likely to continue reading? A short, plain statement of the issue tells the reader what the writing is about and provides context for the discussion that follows.

Make that statement the first paragraph in almost anything you write.

Rule 4
State the Facts Succinctly

Remember that you have already put the issue up front in 75 or fewer words. Now when you put in more facts, the reader will know where the facts fit.

You have already told the reader what the issue is and what you want the reader to do, if anything, in your 75-word statement. Then expand on that. A facts statement of two or three pages should suffice for any issue.

Have someone else (perhaps a teenager) read your facts statement and see if that reader can tell you what the facts are. Maybe the technical details won't be clear, but the facts should be clear to anyone, whether or not they are in your industry or discipline.

Be concise. Advertising and speech writers know that strong writing comes from paring words to a minimum. The fewer the words, the more memorable the point:

> "I have nothing to offer but blood, tears, toil, and sweat."
> "I have a dream."
> "Where's the beef?"

Rule 5
Avoid Overchronicling — Most Dates Are Clutter

There is nothing wrong with stating the facts in chronological order. But do not fall into the habit of starting every sentence with a date.

Avoid overchronicling. Too much writing contains extraneous dates: "On March 23, 2000, this happened, then on May 6, 2000, this happened." This approach confuses the readers, because we don't know what facts are important, and what, if any, dates we should remember. As a general rule, most dates are not important.

Putting in an exact date signals to the reader that *this date is important — remember it — you will need it later.*

Unless an exact date is important — and sometimes it might be — leave it out. Instead, tell us only the material facts, and why they are important.

You can maintain continuity and order by clues like *next* and *later*, or *next month*. You will be surprised how much better your story flows.

Say *in June* rather than on *June 14, 2006*. It is the specific dates that are the problem. And remember that *June 2006* does not take a comma.

Rule 6
No Parenthetical Numerals

Especially irritating is the practice of spelling out numbers and then attaching parenthetical numericals—a habit learned when scribes used quill pens to copy documents. The real reason for this was to prevent fraud by making it difficult to alter documents. But our laser printers are unlikely to print *four* instead of *seven.*

Lawyers are the worst at this. They commonly write "There are four (4) plaintiffs and six (6) defendants, all claiming the ten thousand dollars ($10,000). But only three (3) of the four (4) plaintiffs are entitled to recover from one (1) defendant."

The reader automatically repeats the numbers. It is extremely hard to read and looks silly. Unless you are writing your document in longhand—and unless you believe someone will alter your numbers—skip this aggravating habit.

But it's not only lawyers. This distracting nonsense has crept into all kinds of writing. In your next Sunday paper, look at the coupons. You'll probably see something like this:

Do we think that without the parentheticals the reader would be confused? My guess is that the ad department had to "run it by legal" and that the legal department, being composed of lawyers, inserted the numbers. Ugh.

Most coupons have these superfluous words or numbers, but some companies (Procter & Gamble is one) have clear ones. (Maybe they didn't go through the legal department—or they had lawyers who know about plain English.)

This is my favorite good example:

Do we think consumers will be confused by the lack of the *(one)*? Will the cashier still take it?

Another hint about numbers: some stylebooks direct you to write out numbers up to ten, or 20, or even 100. Unless you have a particular style you are required to follow, use words for up to ten, and numbers for 11 and above.

Rule 7
Headings are Signposts— They Should Inform

As part of the "container" you are building in the reader's mind, have headings that tell the reader what is coming. Headings should convey information. "Facts" is better than no heading, but it conveys no information. "The Problem with Widgets" tells the reader the nature of the facts that are coming. "Conclusion" is better that nothing, but "We can save $560,000" conveys information—and grabs the reader's attention.

Headings are signposts that guide the reader. If your document is one page you may not need to break it up; but if it is longer, separate it into numbered headings. And why not use the headings to inform or persuade?

Headings do not just give context, they also signal the reader when to safely take a break. The reader needs breaks in digesting complex material. Separate the parts— and subparts—into headings. And use a sans serif font for headings (See Rule 9).

How many should there be? There is no set rule, but I wouldn't go more than two pages of double-spaced type or one page of single-spaced without a heading.

Examples:

I. The Fire and the Aftermath
II. The Problem with Widgets
III. We can save $560,000
IV. The Proposed Pricepoints
V. Why we need new software

Notice that in some examples most words are capitalized and some not. This is a style choice you can make. But be consistent.

Rule 8
Write Short Paragraphs

Short paragraphs give the reader a chance to pause and digest what has gone before. Just like headings and short sentences, short paragraphs provide a break. If you put three or four sentences with new information in each paragraph, that is enough. Long paragraphs are daunting. Here is an example:

> The general aim of this conference, if I understand its theme correctly, is to explore the relationship of philosophy and its history. There are two fundamental positions that have been adopted with respect to this issue by philosophers. The first denies that there is or that there should be any relation between them. Those who favor this perspective point out that whatever philosophers do and/or accomplish is irrelevant to what historians do and/or accomplish, and vice versa. For example, they ask: What could what Thales thought about the basic stuff of which the world is made have to do with current questions of philosophy? Indeed, arguing from analogy, they note that no serious astronomer today pays any attention to what Ptolemy thought about the heavens, so why should a contemporary philosopher pay attention to Thales or Aristotle? According to this point of

view, there is nothing relevant that the history of philosophy can contribute to philosophy. Something similar could be said concerning the contribution of philosophy to its history. For, so the argument goes, how could contemporarily developed concepts and ideas help in the proper understanding of concepts and ideas developed in a different age and context? Historians of philosophy, then, have no need for philosophy as such.

The average reader will balk at tackling such a long paragraph. Breaking it up would allow much better communication.

The writing is not really bad, but the reader's eyes glaze over before attempting to read this paragraph. Some readers will just skip such a long paragraph.

There is no rule on how many sentences should be in a paragraph. Usually three or four is enough. A paragraph is supposed to be one thought. But you can break the thoughts into smaller pieces.

And you can have a one-sentence paragraph—for emphasis.

Remember each new piece of information should build on the old. You may have seen paragraphs diagrammed so that each sentence refers back to something in the last sentence. That is called building on context—building on prior knowledge.

Put a topic sentence first in each paragraph. This is another form of putting context before detail. Tell the reader what the paragraph is about before adding details. Some people skim by reading only the first sentence of each paragraph—if they do, they will still get the important points.

Rule 9
Form is Important—
Make it Look Good

Obviously, the substance of your writing is most important—but to communicate the substance, use the best form possible. If you go to a presentation and the speaker is dressed badly, and late, you will tend to discount what the speaker has to say. Same with writing. If it looks bad it has less credibility.

It is so much easier nowadays to make the document look good. Some of us remember the old days of typewriters—there were only two type styles, and margins were difficult to change. Now our documents can look great! On standard 8.5 x 11 paper, use at least one-inch margins—margins of 1.25 or 1.3 are even better. And use an easy-to-read typeface. You would be surprised how much difference it makes in readability.

Just about the most unreadable font is `Courier`. It is a monospaced type, meaning that each letter takes up the same space. That was necessary in typewriter days, because each letter had to fit the same size space. But even then, when we wanted something more readable, we used a typesetter and printer. Did you ever see a book printed in `Courier`? Of course not.

Now, we can do the printing from our desk; but we do not always get it right. For example, I have seen firms spend hundreds of thousands of dollars on technology only to make their documents look like they were typed on a 1940 Underwood. Never use `Courier`.

Use a serif type for text—serifs are the dohickeys on type. Note the "tail" on the a. The serifs have a function: the serifs direct the reader's eyes to the next letter. We read horizontally, so the serifs help the flow. A serif type is always best for text.

Times New Roman is the standard now, probably because Microsoft selected it as the default font on Word. (The first default was Courier!) But you don't have to follow Microsoft everywhere.

One problem with Times New Roman is that the punctuation marks, especially periods and commas, are too small. That is because the type was designed for the *London Times*. In a newspaper, the ink bleeds to make the letters, and the periods and commas, bigger. But on our laser printers, the periods and commas don't bleed. And the reader needs to see the periods—which the English call full stops.

Times is also a very condensed type. It is harder on the eyes. Other examples of serif fonts are **Georgia**, Garamond (I find that Garamond prints too lightly), Book Antiqua, and Palatino. This book is in Palatino. Georgia was designed for the Internet, so is much more readable—it's also bigger. Our court now uses 11.5-point Georgia. Of the commonly available (and free) fonts, I recommend Georgia or Palatino for text. That is for text that takes some time to read. If you are doing a one-paragraph memo, the gain in readability is not great, so you can use something different. But for more lengthy text, always use a serif type.

A non-serif, or sans serif, type is good for headings because it directs the reader's eyes downward to the material following the heading. Arial, Tahoma, and Verdana are common sans serif typefaces. Use one of those or a similar font for titles and headings.

And do not use ALL CAPITALS. Even though all capitals are bigger, they are much more difficult to read than capitals and lowercase letters. That is because we are used to seeing the letters that go above the line, b, d, h, f, k, l, t, k—and ones that go below—g, p, q, y, j. Part of our reading is making out the letters by their shape. All caps negates this.

If you want to emphasize, use **bold** or *italics*, but use either very sparingly—you want your words and sentences themselves to provide emphasis, not artificial devices. Technically, italics are harder to read, so bold is better for emphasis.

This is one area where you can occasionally deviate from the rules. In a brochure or a sign, you can be more creative. Sometimes, different typefaces are acceptable; but if you are going to use a fancy face, know why you are doing it.

In formal papers, stick to the basics. If you are doing a brochure or a presentation document, you can experiment more. Those documents typically don't contain large blocks of text, so readability isn't as much of an issue. But beware of overdesign.

The advent of desktop publishing brought forth too many newsletters and brochures that have the kitchen-sink approach to graphic design—using too many boxes, shapes, and colors. Keep it simple. Don't do many different colors, graphics, and pictures unless they add meaning. More often than not, they are just distracting. For design projects, hire a professional graphic designer. But still beware of too much clutter.

Rule 10
Edit, Edit, Edit

Edit, edit, edit, and edit again. Typos, bad grammar, and misplaced paragraphs (which were not such a problem before word processing) simply take away from your credibility.

Keep a copy of Bryan Garner's book *A Dictionary of Modern American Usage* at your side to answer grammar, syntax, and punctuation questions. It is indispensible. Though it's a reference book, it is so good that you might just read it.

With new technology always comes new pitfalls—following the "spellcheck" or "grammarcheck" blindly leads to some weird words and constructions. If you have a staff member do the word processing, it is even more important to read every word. Spellcheck can substitute wrong words—words spelled correctly, but not what you mean.

You may mean *constitution*, but spellcheck reads it as *constipation*. And don't even think of the *penal* system or the *public* interest.

Those of us who do our own writing—or edit by computer—should always do a final edit—do not let your assistant do the final edit with spellcheck without proofing very carefully again. Then, have someone who is not involved proofread again. Proofing our own writing doesn't always work—we tend to see what we think we have written.

The 1818 Rule

Rule 11
Write Short Sentences — the 1818 Rule Part I

Write short, crisp sentences. What is the most underused punctuation mark in most writing? The period — it is that key down at the lower right of your keyboard. The most overused is easy — the comma.

You should strive to average 18 words per sentence, or fewer — hence the *18*, the first part of the 1818 Rule. If you have 19 or 20 words per sentence, you are still okay, but if you get much over 20, you are sacrificing readability.

Long sentences are difficult to read. The reader sometimes forgets what the first part of a long sentence said by the end. I was tempted to use legal examples here, because they are so common. William Howard Taft once used a 328-word sentence. But these are from business writing.

The following is just a random example:

> The first main prevention method that can help our company eliminate employee theft is to perform pre-employment screening of all applicants for positions with our company, which can be a major aid for all of us in the hiring process because it will either decrease the amount of theft or even increase it if we are not careful in hiring. We need to hire applicants for positions who have the proper work skills required for the positions and for being successful in their jobs and who have job-related values in areas such as integrity, service, and safety to ensure that there is less chance that they will engage in employee theft, which is why we need to use pre-employment screening techniques that identify job candidates who do not possess the qualities of integrity, service, and safety, as demonstrated in their past job performance or criminal records.

Gosh. Just two sentences totaling 146-words. Or how about this one:

> This relates to our informal discussion on December 1 about your poor timekeeping and I now understand from your manager that your initial improvement has not been sustained and that, over the last month, your punctuality and attendance have been of an unacceptable level so I am now moving on to the first formal stage of the Disciplinary Procedure, a copy of which is attached for yourself.

Sixty-seven words in one sentence. It could be translated into this:

> On December 1, we talked about your poor timekeeping. Your manager says that you didn't keep up your initial improvement. Over the last month, your punctuality and attendance have not been acceptable, so I am now moving on to the first formal stage of the Disciplinary Procedure. I attach a copy for you.

Now it's 53 words, and, more important, 13 words per sentence. And note the *for you*, rather than *for yourself*. (Thanks to Bill DuBay, of Impact Information, for these examples and the translation.)

Long sentences are especially difficult when strung together. Sophisticated readers can understand longer sentences—up to maybe 40 words if they are properly constructed—but no one can wade through ten in a row. Break up the pace—follow a longer sentence with a short one.

How do you check your average sentence length? In Word, call up Spellcheck. On the bottom you will see "Options." Click on that and another screen will come up. The last box will say "Show Readability Statistics." Check that box and at the end of Spellcheck each time it will tell you the words per sentence—along with the percentage of passive-voice sentences, which we will get to next.

And while you are there, tell it that you want two spaces between sentences, commas and periods inside of quotes, and kill the dumb part that stops you from using *and* or *but* to start a sentence. (More on both issues later.)

One exception to the "long sentence" rule: lists. People understand lists, especially if they are bulleted. See Rule 23 for some pointers on lists.

Rule 12
Use Mainly Active Voice — the 1818 Rule Part II

Passive voice results from the use of a *be* verb: be, is, was, and the like. Make sure your document has no more than 18% passive-voice sentences.

Passive voice is not forbidden. Sometimes you do not need to name the actor — *Many books have been written about widgets.* Or a smooth transition from one sentence to the next requires you to put the subject first. Or you might want to hide the actor — *Mistakes were made.*

If you are a lawyer or insurance adjuster for the truck driver who ran over the nun in the crosswalk, you will not write it that way. You'll write, *An accident occurred.* That takes the actor (your bad guy) out of the action.

But usually active is better; action is easier to understand. We do not usually talk in passive voice.

Closely related to passive voice is nominalization. Sometimes we take a perfectly good verb and make it into a noun, burying the verb in the sentence. And it usually results in a passive-voice sentence — a form of *to be* becomes the verb.

Sometimes it just adds a verb and obscures the real verb.

Instead of a straightforward, *The police searched Smith,* we might say, *The police performed a search upon Smith.* Is the performance what we want to stress? Of course not; it's the search. Searched is a fine verb—it conveys exactly what happened. When we muck it up with a performance, it is at least distracting—at most misleading.

And when we write, S*mith conducted a study of widgets,* we really don't mean to emphasize the *conducted.* If we write, *Smith studied widgets,* it makes much more sense and is shorter. You *applied* for the job, instead of *filed* (or *made) an application.*

Most nominalizations end with *-tion, -ment, -ence, -ance, -ure, -ery.*

Verb	**Noun**
determine	determination
advance	advancement
modify	modification
improve	improvement
affirm	affirmance
divest	divestiture
agree	agreement
admit	admittance
depend	dependence

Nominalizations not only add a noun-verb, they also add an article. So you have two extra words, in addition to taking the action out of the sentence.

Verb	Noun
moved	made a motion
applied	filed an application
produce	commence production
assumed	made an assumption
save	result in a savings
prefer	have a preference
violates	is in violation
reduce	make a reduction

Dr. Terri Mester, an English professor at Case Western, uses examples of nominalization in her plain-writing seminars (her seminars are worthwhile, as are mine). This is my favorite Mester sentence, with the nominalizations and passives italicized. "Although *there are* no new natural gas areas that *will be* created, an *enhancement* of land use through *reduction* in flooding *is obtained* through the plan."

How about this: "The plan creates no new natural gas areas, but reducing flooding enhances land use." The active-voice revision strikes out 12 useless words (46% of the sentence).

Another of Dr. Mester's examples (all used by permission): "If there is a continuation of this breach, my client will effect an immediate termination of the contract." Revised: "If this breach continues, my client will terminate the contract." This version eliminates eight superfluous words (44%) and strengthens the sentence.

Hunt down passive voice and nominalization. If there is no good reason for using it, put your sentence back the way real people would talk. A number of examples are in the table in Rule 16.

Here is a particularly bad example of governmentese. It is all in passive, has nominalizations and jargon, plus other errors. The reader must try to translate into English.

> This Phase I draft report of the Goods Movement Action Plan does not include prioritized infrastructure project recommendations or prioritized environmental mitigation strategies. It is a foundational document that details key California goods movement issues, including: projections of future growth, characterization of environmental impacts, an unprioritized inventory of mitigation strategies, characterization of transportation corridors, an unprioritized inventory of pending and proposed infrastructure projects, and a discussion of key public safety and homeland security issues.

It is from The California Business, Transportation and Housing Agency and the California Environmental Protection Agency's "Draft Goods Movement Action Plan."

Mike Durant, of the plain-English website CalClarity, translates it for us:

> This draft plan is about how we move goods around the state and ways to make sure we protect the environment as we try to improve our roads, seaports, and airports. In no particular order, it details environmental, safety, and security problems we need to solve so we can move goods faster and safer.

Now it makes sense. When you avoid passive voice and nominalization you make it easier on the reader.

Rule 13
Use *But* and *And* to Begin Sentences

Do not be afraid to start sentences with *and* or *but*. This signifies good writing. The reason your grammar-school teacher told you not to start a sentence with *and* was because you wrote, *I have a mother. And a father. And a dog.* These are not sentences. So the teacher used a shorthand "rule" and told you not to start a sentence with *and*.

There is not and never has been such a grammar rule. Bryan Garner calls these grammar non-rules "superstitions." Even Microsoft's spellcheck is wrong. But you can turn that part off. Do so.

Use *but* rather than *however* to start a sentence, and see how much better it reads.

For many reasons, you should not begin a sentence with *however*. First, there are two senses of however: the *but* sense and the *any way* sense—however it goes, you lose. Sometimes the reader has to back up to get the meaning. Even worse, *however* requires a comma, which is a pause—why would you want to start a sentence with a break before you get to the second word? *But* does not require a comma.

Almost any example of good writing pulled at random will contain numerous examples of this rule. *The Wall*

Street Journal and *The New York Times* are well-written—look at the front page of either and circle the number of sentences beginning with *and* or *but*. There will be three to ten. You didn't notice before, precisely because it was good writing.

> Look at Oliver Wendell Holmes Jr, for example:
>
> Courts proceed step by step. And we now have to consider whether the cautious statement in the former case marked the limit of the law.
>
> But to many people the superfluous is necessary, and it seems to me that Government does not go beyond its sphere in attempting to make life livable for them.

Just randomly look at writings you consider good, and you will find countless examples.

James Joyce:

> But the man could not hear with the noise of the furnace. It was just as well.

Tom Wolfe:

> He had grown up associating religion with the self-delusion and aimlessness of adults. But now he thought about the soul, *his* soul. Or he tried to. But it was only a word!

Faulkner:

> But it was not for him, not yet. The humility was there; he had learned that. And he could learn patience.

Melville:

> But on board the seventy-four in which Billy now swung his hammock, very little in the manner of the men and nothing obvious in the demeanor of the officers would have suggested to an ordinary observer that the Great Mutiny was a recent event.

Shakespeare:

> Thou hadst, and more, Miranda. But how is it
> That this lives in thy mind? What seeth thou else
> In the dark backward and abysm of time?

Asimov:

> But it would be silly to wear clothes in the rain. You didn't wear clothes in the shower. If it rained, you would take off your clothes. That would be the only thing that made sense.

Shakespeare again:

> But I am very sorry, good Horatio
> That to Laertes I forgot myself;

> For, by the image of my cause, I see
> The portraiture of his: I'll court his favours.
> But, sure, the bravery of his grief did put me
> Into a towering passion.[4]

If you need even more to convince a backward colleague, just look in any book or article that your colleague admits is good writing. Or flip through anything by Tom Wolfe, Herman Melville, Isaac Asimov, or any good writer. You will find *ands* and *buts* at the beginning of many sentences.

Rule 14
Distinguish Between *That* and *Which*

Use *that* restrictively and *which* nonrestrictively. That is, if the clause can stand alone, it is preceded by which. If it cannot stand by itself, *that* is appropriate. (In Commonwealth English, *which* is used both ways.)

Consider the following examples:

We need to begin production, *which* must precede distribution.

The team *that* won the prize is from Sweden.

Our company, *which* was founded in 1889, still occupies its original building.

She made the sale *that* broke the limit.

They were driving a 1997 truck, *which* was in dire need of repair.

The truck *that* they were driving broke down.

Failure to distinguish appropriately is a common error and one that (not which) I have been guilty of on occasion. But I now have it down, I think. Take my word that the distinction is important.

The easy way to remember is that *which* is preceded by a comma; *that* is not. Follow that rule and you will be correct 98% of the time. That's an A.

Some editors have a penchant for removing most *thats*. But it is usually better to keep them in, unless you can remove them without any possibility of confusion.

Rule 15
Use the Dash, Parenthesis, and Comma for Degrees of Emphasis

Though you should avoid cluttering up your document with too many incidental comments, sometimes they fit nicely. A dash provides the greatest emphasis—it is the strongest break. Next in degree is the parenthesis, then the comma. If anything, I have overused dashes in this work. But I find them useful. They make a sentence more readable.

Make sure that you use the correct mark for a dash. A dash on an ancient typewriter was two hyphens (- -). In printing, you never saw two hyphens masquerading as a dash. An *em-dash* (word—word) is the proper punctuation now. Your word processor will convert two hyphens to an *em-dash* if you tell it to. Be sure to program it correctly. In Word, go to tools/autocorrect/options and set two hypens to be a dash. While you are doing that, also make sure to set it for "smart quotes," which are different at the beginning and end of the quotation.

There is also an *en-dash*, which is slightly longer than a hyphen; it is used in constructions like 1880–1890 (contrast 1880-1890 with a hyphen), or the Lincoln–Douglas debates. If you have a resume that says you worked at a certain place from 2001–2006, there should be an *en dash*, not a hyphen between. You really will be ahead of the game if you use the *em-dash* properly—if you cheat and use a hyphen for an *en-dash*, some people won't notice. But a perfectionist would distinguish. The person reading your resume might know the difference—yours may be the only correct one.

Rule 16
One Word is Usually Enough

Don't fall into the lawyer's habit of using two or three or four words for one—*null and void; each and every; devise and bequeath; grant, bargain, sell, and convey; right, title, and interest.*

This goofiness originated with the Norman Conquest in 1066. After that, it was necessary to use both the English and the French words so that all parties could understand. And, of course, "educated" people wrote in Latin, so they sometimes threw that into the mix too.

I always ask lawyers whether they have ever had a client come in for a will (last will and testament) and say, "I'd like to give the *rest* of my estate to my spouse, the *residue* to my daughter, and the *remainder* to my son"? Is there a difference? Of course not. *Rest* would be fine.

If there is no difference between words, don't use more than one. If something is *null*, we assume it is also *void*. If a debt is *due*, it is also *payable*.

A related tendency is to use many words when one is more understandable—*sufficient number of = enough; that point in time = then; for the reason that = because.* A longer list follows.

Here's how to fix some common usages:

BAD	BETTER
the means by which	how
entered a contract to	contracted
filed a motion	moved
filed an application	applied
adequate number of	enough
for the reason that	because
in the event of	if
in light of the fact that	because
notwithstanding the fact that	although
notwithstanding	despite
in order to	to
at this point in time	now
by means of	by
at a later date	later
until such time as	until

BAD	BETTER
during the month of May	in May
whether or not	whether (98% of the time. You only need the "or not" if it's the *regardless* sense: the game will go on *whether or not* it rains)
a distance of five miles	five miles
made a complaint	complained
makes mention of	mentions
utilize	use
period of a week	a week
effectuate	cause
provide assistance	help
is violative of	violates
provide protection to	protect
is of the opinion that	believes
as a consequence of	because of

BAD	BETTER
made provision	provided
with regard to	about
in connection with	with
make a reduction	reduce
each and every	either *each* or *every*
provide responses	respond
offered testimony	testified
reveal the identity of	identify
reach a resolution	resolve
was in conformity with	conformed
effectuate settlement	settle
make inquiry	ask
are in compliance	comply
make allegations	allege
make an examination of	examine

"We have a deal. But both sides put in so many howevers, notwithstandings, and provided thats that I don't know if we really agreed to anything."

Rule 17
Hyphenate Phrasal Adjectives

The reader is confused by nouns acting as adjectives, or by two adjectives together modifying one noun. Often, the reader will have to back up and read again.

Sentences like these fool the reader:

The widget repair mechanism . . .
A desk bound boss . . .
The public policy exception . . .
The law abiding citizen . . .

The reader may be fooled into thinking that *the public* or *the law* are the subjects of the sentences, rather than modifiers of the actual subjects, *exception* and *citizen*. The reader sometimes has to back up and reread. Just add a hyphen (*the widget-repair mechanism, the public-policy exception*), and the reader knows that the hyphenated words are modifiers.

Words that end in *-ly* are not hyphenated, because they are adverbs—or because the *-ly* tells the reader that the word is a modifier, not a noun.

Always hyphenate phrases like *wrongful-discharge suit*, or *desk-bound boss*. Take my word for it—the hyphens increase readability.

Rule 18
Always Question *Of*

Write *the company's profit*, not *the profit of the company*. There is nothing wrong with the possessive. Somewhere, someone told someone not to use possessives, maybe because *docket of the court* sounds more formal than *the court's docket*. It is not. It is just clutter—and much harder to read.

Use the "find" feature on your word processor to hunt down these awkward constructions. Some uses of *of* are fine, but usually, if the word is possessive, just make it so with an apostrophe.

A possessive is fine, as long as the idea is possessive. But a possessive is different than a plural. In the last decade or so, many people seem to have fallen into the "creeping apostrophe." This phenomenon does not do away with an *of*; it just adds an apostrophe for no reason, making all plurals into possessives.

Some (real) examples:

Hot Dog's for Sale
Smith & Co., Surveyor's
Hamburger's $1.99
Happy Hour on Friday's

Tuxedo's on Sale
Hanaford & Sons, Architect's
Taxi's Only
Cocktail's
Heavenly Beam's Church

Rule 19
Use the Serial Comma

In a list of three or more, always insert the serial comma. Some writers insist on omitting the last comma, before the "and" or "or." Never omit the last comma—doing so can cause misinterpretation.

Chickens, ducks, and geese is clear. *Chickens, ducks and geese*, allows someone—a salesperson, a lawyer, or judge—to assert that *ducks and geese* are a distinct category. Or consider *Smith ordered bacon, eggs and cheese*. Did Smith want eggs mixed with cheese? If you write *Smith ordered bacon, eggs, and cheese* the meaning is clear.

Many court cases discuss the problems created by leaving out the serial comma. In some, the court had to search code sections near the legislation in question to determine what, if any, rule the drafter followed. In others, the lack of a serial comma created confusion. In another, the "rule of the serial comma" was debated page after page by a panel of judges.

Using the serial comma never creates ambiguity, leaving it out sometimes does. So why would you use a construction that is by its nature ambiguous? This is a rule that you may not break.

Rule 20
Avoid Unnecessary Preambles

Cut useless preambles. A preamble usually consists of useless or "throat-clearing" words. In speaking, preambles are not usually harmful—you are giving the listener time to digest. But it writing, unnecessary preambles can weaken or hide the point they introduce. And they add nothing except distraction.

Here are some unnecessary preambles:

Let it be emphasized . . .
It is important to add that . . .
It may be recalled that . . .
It is of significance that . . .
It is interesting to note that . . .
In this regard . . .
Let me say this about that . . .

These phrases add nothing but clutter. In speaking, this type of transition is sometimes necessary to give the listener a break. But it never is in writing.

Further, some of these even cause backlash from the reader. If you say something is important, the reader may be tempted to disagree. And if you say, "it may be recalled," you're telling the readers you think they're so stupid they can't remember what you said two pages ago.

Rule 21
You May Split Infinitives—But Not Often

Usually, an infinitive—a verb phrase containing *to*—should not be split. That is, the *to* should immediately precede the verb: *to exit quickly* rather than *to quickly exit*. But you may freely split the infinitive if your ear tells you it is okay—or if the meaning is different.

What is the most famous split infinitive? *To boldly go where no one has gone before.* It would be weaker if we unsplit the infinitive: *To go boldly.* The former is stronger. Just use your ear. But if you are not sure of your ear, always prefer the unsplit infinitive.

Never splitting infinitives is just another bogus "rule." Merriam Webster's online dictionary: "Even though there has never been a rational basis for objecting to the split infinitive, the subject has become a fixture of folk belief about grammar."

Rule 22
Commas and Periods Inside Quotes—Always

Quotation marks are wrongly placed in so much writing. And it's a glaring error. Nary a day goes by that I don't find mistakes in quotation marks.

In American English, all commas and periods go inside the quotation marks. Always. Exclamation points and question marks go inside if part of the quote, outside if not. This is true whether the quotation is a whole sentence or a fragment.

WRONG	RIGHT
Williams believes that "might makes right".	Williams believes that "might makes right."
Smith said, "I am not going", and stayed seated.	Smith said, "I am not going," and stayed seated.
The author wrote: "We cannot abide consistency".	The author wrote: "We cannot abide consistency."

In Commonwealth English, the opposite is true. So if you see a Canadian, British, Pakistani, Indian, South African, New Zealand, or Australian quotation, the periods and commas follow the same rule as the one below for question marks and exclamation points.

But we are in America—you must get it right. An easy way to check, if you don't have this or Garner's book handy, is to simply look at a book printed in the United States. I have never seen a professional book editor get it wrong; but it's a whole different story with memos, brochures, ads, and videos.

By their nature, colons and semicolons go outside the end of a quote, even if the original had a colon or a semicolon in that position.

WRONG	RIGHT
The court quotes Shakespeare: "To be or not to be;" it then overruled the objection.	The court quotes Shakespeare: "To be or not to be"; it then overruled the objection.

The only time you have to make a decision where punctuation goes is when you have a question mark or an exclamation point. Remember, these go inside the quote marks if they are part of the quotation, outside if they are not.

WRONG	RIGHT
Smith said, "Get Help"! and ran.	Smith said, "Get Help!" and ran.
The boss said, "My options are more equal than your options!"	The boss said, "My options are more equal than your options"! (assuming the emphasis is yours, not the boss's.)
The judge asked: "Are you ready for trial"?	The judge asked: "Are you ready for trial?"

Notice above that short quotations may be introduced by either a colon or a comma. Prefer the colon when (1) it introduces something more formal or something said in a formal atmosphere, and (2) the source is identified before the colon. If you do not want to have to remember that suggestion (it is not a rule), then you will not be wrong if you always use a comma.

Sometimes the quote can simply be part of the sentence, usually preceded by that: We all know that "no good deed goes unpunished." This formulation requires no additional punctuation.

Other punctuation can be tricky as well. Garner's book

has a whole section on punctuation. I find it helpful to read through it every couple months.

Possessives and plural possessives have always given me trouble. Most possessives just add an apostrophe followed by an s. *Roger's hat.* This is so even if the original word is plural: *men's room.* Or if the word ends in an s: *Jones's dog.* The only time you can make a possessive by adding only an apostrophe is when the name is Biblical or from antiquity and ends in s: *Jesus', Aristophanes'.*

Since this is not a grammar book, we'll end it there. But make sure you consult Garner's book if you have the slightest doubt.

Rule 23
Use Lists to Simplify

Using lists can improve readability by cutting sentence length and ousting duplication. People understand lists. They are used to seeing them. Consider the following paragraph from a court brief:

> Jones sets forth three reasons for the assignment. First, Jones contends that Smith was the best person for the job because she had the proper training. Second, Jones contends that Smith was the best person for the job because she was free to move. Third, Jones asserts that Smith was the best person for the job because she had seniority.

See how much better it reads this way:

> Jones contends that Smith was the best person for the job because she had (1) proper training; (2) freedom to move; and (3) seniority.

We have cut the number of words by almost two-thirds—21 versus 60. And we have gained, not lost, meaning.

One trick is to try to get as much as possible on the left. That is, see how much of the phrasing can be used only once.

And when you have a list of more than a few entries, drop down with bullets or numbers, depending on whether the order is important. Use numbers if the sequence matters, bullets if it doesn't.

Rule 24
Use the Possessive Before Gerunds

A gerund is a verb converted to a noun by adding an *-ing*. Gerunds should not be confused with participles—verbs converted to adjectives by adding the *-ing*. Gerunds take a possessive form of the preceding noun or pronoun; participles do not.

The suspect's fleeing the scene was foolhardy. (F*leeing* is a gerund—it requires a possessive.)

The suspect fleeing the scene was shot. (*Fleeing* here is an adjective describing suspect, so no possessive.)

Personal pronouns especially require this construction.

I appreciate your helping me with the project.

My fondest memory of that trip was my meeting Sam.

The problem was his dozing at work.

But use your ear. Some words do not take the possessive, such as words that already end in *s*.

The members were upset at the thought of the ducks being killed.

Most often, though, the possessive should be used before the gerund. Put in the apostrophe, and sound out the sentence.

His taking the course was a good idea.

Smith's holding that office was temporary.

The professor was shocked by his making the grade.

This rule is not absolute, but good writers follow it. Sloppy writers do not.

Rule 25
Remember the Reader

We touched on this in an earlier rule, but I have come to believe it is important enough to separate into a freestanding rule. Put yourself in the reader's place. Look through your reader's spectacles, not yours.

Keep in mind that you know all about what you are writing; and the reader generally knows little before reading your document. You know what you want to convey (we hope). The reader has no idea of your message unless you can convey it.

Even if you have followed all the rules, leave your work aside a day or two and read it through again. And have a a friend or colleague read it to see if it makes sense. It's difficult to correct our own writing because we see what we expect to see.

Be sure to put your document through the readability calculations of your word-processing program. It will tell you the grade level, the percentage of passive-voice sentences, and the average sentence length. (Remember the 1818 Rule.) These figures are not totally accurate, but they will give you a rough idea of the degree of difficulty the reader will encounter.

If the document tests too high, revise it. Hint: two ways to improve the readability score: (1) getting the passive voice out, and (2) using easier words (don't use big words to show you are smart—use only words your reader will understand). But the first and easiest way to raise readability is to use shorter sentences. Improve your work by having more periods run through it.

We Can Do Better

This book is only a start. I hope you have picked up a few points that [not *which*] will improve your writing.

The books in the bibliography are my favorites, but there are, and will be, many others. Though I may disagree with a few points in some writing books, almost all agree on the basics—shorter sentences, shorter paragraphs, no pompous words, fewer passive sentences.

We have talked a lot about form. Dressing your message in the best clothes will not make it eloquent; it will only make it presentable. Remember, the form is not everything, but it is very important. The medium is not the message; the message is the message. But if the message is not conveyed to the reader, it is not even a message. A report with bad type, grammatical mistakes, and long paragraphs and sentences might not even be read!

The turning of words into a product—a report, a letter, a memo—is not a job of easy assembly. It is an art. And the more vivid our colors, the sharper our images, the more effective our art. The message is the message—but we must make it as clear and vibrant as we know how.

Write well!

Bibliography

Books

Garner, Bryan A. *Garner's Modern American Usage.* New York: Oxford University Press, 2003

Strunk, William Jr. and E. B. White. *The Elements of Style* (4th Ed). Needham Heights, MA: Allen & Bacon,1999)

Williams, Joseph M. *Style: Ten Lessons in Clarity and Grace* (8th Ed). White Plains, NY: Longman, 2004

Biography

MARK P. PAINTER was elected to the Ohio First District Court of Appeals in 1994 and re-elected without opposition since. For the previous 13 years, Judge Painter served on the Hamilton County Municipal Court.

A Cincinnati native, Judge Painter attended the University of Cincinnati, where he was elected Student Body President in 1969, receiving a B.A. in 1970, and a J.D. in 1973. He practiced law for nine years before becoming a judge, mainly with a firm that later became part of Thompson Hine.

Judge Painter is recognized as an outstanding legal scholar. As a municipal court judge, he was the most-published trial judge in Ohio. More than 350 of Judge Painter's decisions have been published nationally, making him one of the most-published judges in Ohio history. One of his decisions was named one of the six best in the nation for 2005.

In addition to this book, he is the author of *Ohio Driving Under the Influence Law* (WestGroup, now in its 16th edition), the only legal textbook on DUI in Ohio. His book *The Legal Writer* (Jarndyce & Jarndyce Press) is now in its third edition. He is coauthor of *Ohio Appellate Practice* (WestGroup). Judge Painter has also written more than 120 articles for various publications.

He has written a biography, *William Howard Taft: President & Chief Justice* (Jarndyce & Jarndyce Press, 2004). He is currently working on a biography of Warren G. Harding.

As an Adjunct Professor at the University of Cincinnati College of Law from 1990 to 2006, Judge Painter taught agency and partnership and advanced legal writing.

He teaches DUI law, appellate practice, legal writing, and legal ethics to judges and lawyers throughout the country. He has lectured at more than 175 seminars across the country for, among others, the Ohio Judicial College, the National Institute of Trial Advocacy, Professional Education Systems Institute, The Kroger Company, Nationwide, and the Ohio State Bar Association.

Judge Painter has served as a Trustee of the Cincinnati Freestore/Foodbank, the Cincinnati Bar Association, the Friends of the William Howard Taft Birthplace, and the Citizens School Committee. He is a Master of the Bench Emeritus of the Potter Stewart Inn of Court, and served for three years as a member of the Ohio Supreme Court Board of Commissioners on Grievances and Discipline.

Judge Painter is a member of the Cincinnati, Ohio State, and American Bar Associations, the American Society of Writers on Legal Subjects (Scribes), the Plain Language International Network, the Legal Writing Institute, Clarity, and the American Judicature Society.

Painter has lived in the Cincinnati neighborhood of Clifton Heights-Fairview for more than 42 years. Mark and his wife, Sue Ann Painter (the author of *William Henry Harrison: Father of the West* and *Architecture in Cincinnati: An Illustrated History of Designing and Building an American City*), were married in 1986.

Judge Painter conducts writing seminars for firms, corporations, and bar associations throughout the country. For information, please contact him through the website below.

www.judgepainter.org